This Is the Lunch That Jesus Served

This Is the
Lunch That
Jesus Served

by Dandi Daley Mackall
Illustrated by Benrei Huang

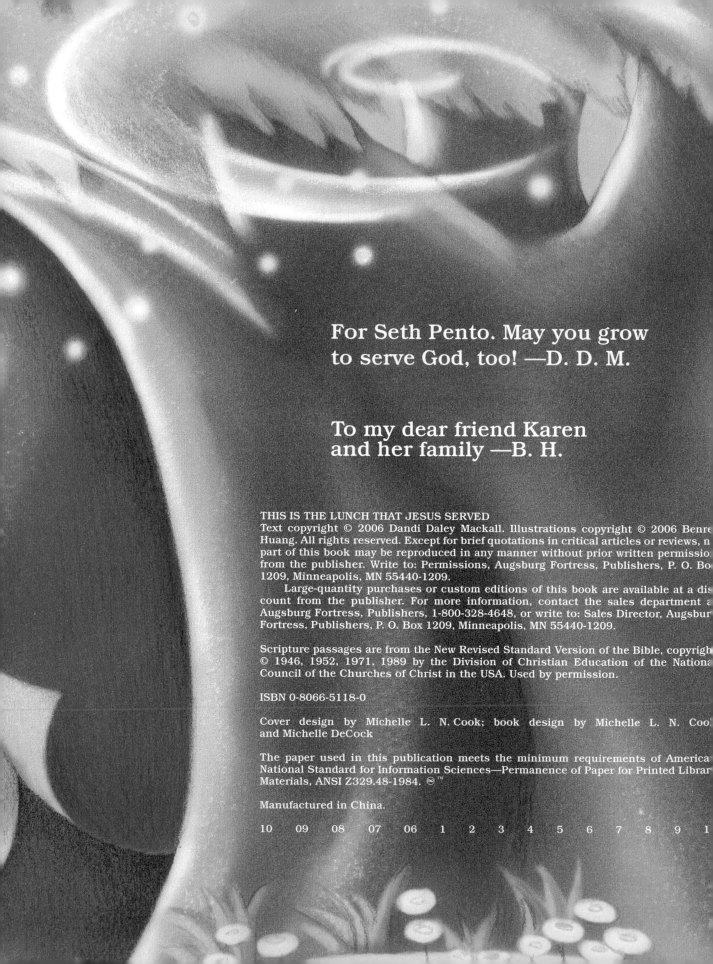

For Seth Pento. May you grow
to serve God, too! —D. D. M.

To my dear friend Karen
and her family —B. H.

This is the lunch
that Jesus served.

This is the boy,
who brought the lunch
that Jesus served.

This is the bread,
brought by the boy,
who gave up the lunch
that Jesus served.

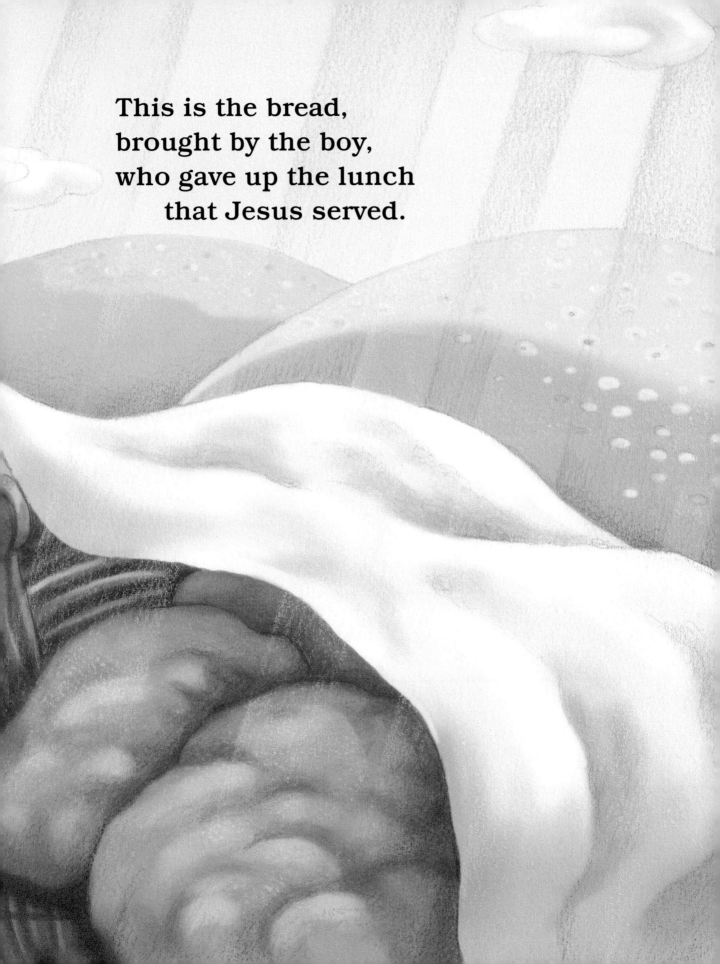

These are the fish
that went with the bread,
brought by the boy,
who gave up the lunch
that Jesus served.

This is the dish
that carried the fish
that went with the bread,
brought by the boy,
who gave up the lunch
that Jesus served.

This is the Man from Galilee,
who blessed the dish
that carried the fish
that went with the bread,
brought by the boy,
who gave up the lunch
    that Jesus served.

These are disciples beside the sea,
who followed the Man from Galilee,
who blessed the dish
that carried the fish
that went with the bread,
brought by the boy,
who gave up the lunch
    that Jesus served.

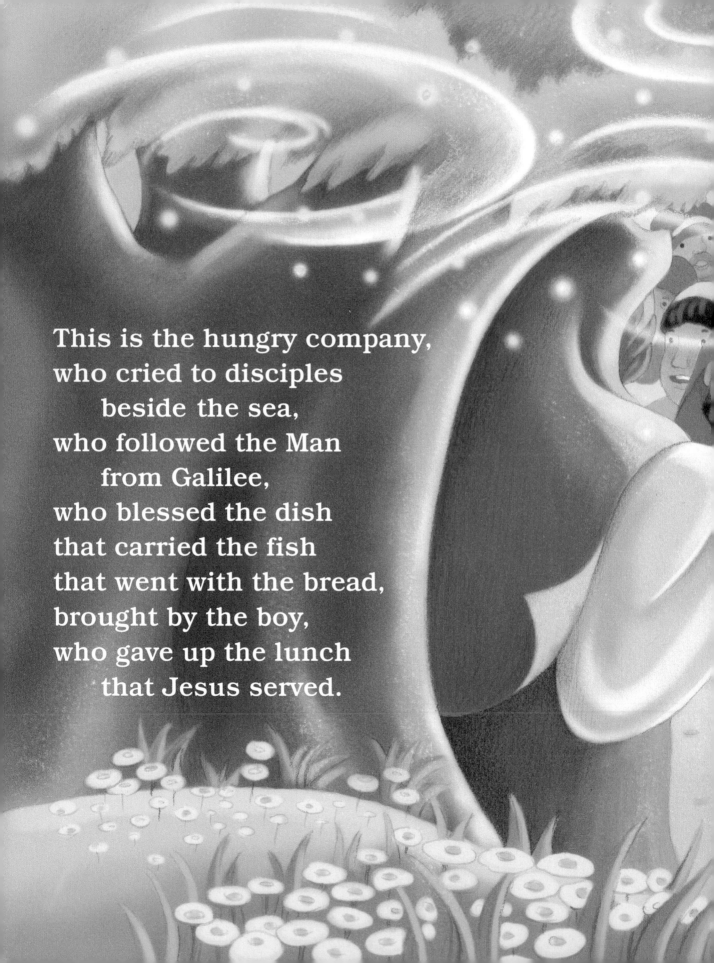

This is the hungry company,
who cried to disciples
    beside the sea,
who followed the Man
    from Galilee,
who blessed the dish
that carried the fish
that went with the bread,
brought by the boy,
who gave up the lunch
    that Jesus served.

These are the baskets, *1, 2, 3,*
passed to the hungry company,
who cried to disciples beside the sea,
who followed the Man from Galilee,
who blessed the dish
that carried the fish
that went with the bread,
brought by the boy,
who gave up the lunch
    that Jesus served.

"This is a miracle!" all agree,
as baskets multiplied *1, 2, 3,*
passed to the hungry company,
who cried to disciples beside the sea,
who followed the Man from Galilee,

who blessed the dish
that carried the fish
that went with the bread,
brought by the boy,
who gave up the lunch
that Jesus served.

This is the well-fed family,
who cried, "It's a miracle! All agree!"
as baskets multiplied *1, 2, 3,*
passed to the hungry company,
who cried to disciples beside the sea,
who followed the Man from Galilee,
who blessed the dish
that carried the fish
that went with the bread,
brought by the boy,
who gave up the lunch
    that Jesus served.

This is the One, God's Only Son,
Who cares for his children,
    for you and me,
and loved the faithful family,
who cried, "It's a miracle!
    All agree!"
as baskets multiplied *1, 2, 3,*
passed to the hungry company,
who cried to disciples
    beside the sea,
who followed the Man
    from Galilee,
who blessed the dish
that carried the fish
that went with the bread,
brought by the boy,
who gave up the lunch
    that Jesus served.

This book is based on the true story of how Jesus fed a crowd of thousands from only five loaves of bread and two fish, offered to him by a young boy at just the right time. Here's the actual account from the Bible:

John 6:1-13 NRSV

[1]After this Jesus went to the other side of the Sea of Galilee, also called the Sea of Tiberias. [2]A large crowd kept following him, because they saw the signs that he was doing for the sick. [3]Jesus went up the mountain and sat down there with his disciples. [4]Now the Passover, the festival of the Jews, was near. [5]When he looked up and saw a large crowd coming toward him, Jesus said to Philip, "Where are we to buy bread for these people to eat?" [6]He said this to test him, for he himself knew what he was going to do. [7]Philip answered him, "Six months' wages would not buy enough bread for each of

them to get a little. ⁸One of his disciples, Andrew, Simon Peter's brother, said to him, ⁹"There is a boy here who has five barley loaves and two fish. But what are they among so many people?" ¹⁰Jesus said, "Make the people sit down." Now there was a great deal of grass in the place; so they sat down, about five thousand in all. ¹¹Then Jesus took the loaves, and when he had given thanks, he distributed them to those who were seated; so also the fish, as much as they wanted. ¹²When they were satisfied, he told his disciples, "Gather up the fragments left over, so that nothing may be lost." ¹³So they gathered them up, and from the fragments of the five barley loaves, left by those who had eaten, they filled twelve baskets.

Fun Fish Facts

God could have created one type of fish. Instead, God has given us thousands of types of amazing fish, from the whale shark, that can grow to 50 feet long and weigh several tons, to the tiny goby fish, which is lucky if it gets to 1/2 inch long. God loves variety!

Early Christians used the fish symbol as a sign of fellowship. It wasn't always safe to be a follower of Jesus Christ, and early Christians were often arrested, beaten, or killed for their faith. If a Christian met a stranger and wanted to know if that person believed in Christ, the Christian might make an arc like this in the dirt:

If the stranger followed Jesus, too, he or she would make an arc in the other direction:

Put them together, and you had a symbol of a fish:

Another name for the fish symbol is "Ichthus." *Ichthus* is the Greek word for "fish." The fish symbol was scrawled on caves or catacombs to mark safe places where the early Christians could meet. Even today, many Christians enjoy showing the sign of the fish. Look around and you'll find the symbol on everything from necklaces to cars.

Bible Bread Facts

Bread is essential to life, and the Bible uses bread as a symbol for how wonderfully God takes care of us. Here are some examples of bread in the Bible:

• When God's people were hungry in the wilderness, God fed them with bread from heaven, which they called "manna."

> *Exodus 16:4: Then the LORD said to Moses, "I am going to rain bread from heaven for you, and each day the people shall go out and gather enough for that day. In that way I will test them, whether they will follow my instruction or not."*

• Jesus' disciples asked him how to pray, and Jesus showed them, praying what we've come to call the Lord's Prayer.

> *Matthew 6:11: "Give us this day our daily bread."*

• Jesus called himself "The Bread of Life." He meant that he's all we'll ever need.

> *John 6:35: Jesus said to them, "I am the bread of life. Whoever comes to me will never be hungry, and whoever believes in me will never be thirsty."*

• Right before Jesus was crucified, he had a "Last Supper" with his disciples. He gave them bread and used it as a symbol to teach them to trust in him.

> *Matthew 26:26: While they were eating, Jesus took a loaf of bread, and after blessing it he broke it, gave it to the disciples, and said, "Take, eat; this is my body."*

Servant Ideas

God can use whatever you have to offer! Try talking with your family and coming up with new ways to show Christ's love to people around you. Here are some ideas:

- Make a fresh loaf of bread and give it to a neighbor. Then tell your neighbors about the story of the lunch that Jesus served (John 6:1-13).

- Make a trail mix out of fish-shaped crackers, raisins, nuts, and pretzels. Tie a ribbon around a bag full of your fish-and-bread mix and deliver it, along with the story of the loaves and fish.

- Invite a family to dinner, especially a family you've never shared a meal with before. Over a fish and bread dinner, tell them the story of how Jesus fed the five thousand.

- Your family might consider volunteering to help with your church's food or mission center. Or you might want to volunteer to help at a community soup kitchen.